THE AIR OF RELAXATION

SOOTHING LAVENDER

PUBLICATIONS INTERNATIONAL, LTD.

Louis Weber, C.E.O.
Publications International, Ltd.
7373 North Cicero Avenue
Lincolnwood, Illinois 60646

Permissions never granted for commercial purposes.

Manufactured in China.

8 7 6 5 4 3 2 1

ISBN: 0-7853-3415-7

Dawn Baumann Brunke has a degree in massage therapy from the Potomac Institute of Myotherapy and practices aromatherapy. She is editor of *Alaska Wellness* magazine and has authored many articles on holistic healing. Ms. Brunke wrote the introduction and profile text of this publication.

Margaret Anne Huffman is an award-winning writer and journalist. She has authored and co-authored inspirational titles including *Second Wind* and *Simple Wisdom*. She has also contributed to *Graces, Family Celebrations,* and *365 Daily Meditations for Women.* Ms. Huffman's work appears on pages 41 and 47.

Laurel Kallenbach is a freelance writer and poet. She has a master of arts degree in creative writing from Syracuse University and is former senior editor of *Delicious!* magazine. Ms. Kallenbach's work appears on pages 27, 28, 38, 39, 52 and 56.

Katherine Lyons is a professional speaker, writer, and poet. She is founder of "The Society for Ladies Who Laugh Out Loud," a national network of women gathering to rekindle energy, perspective, a sense of humor, and positive focus. Ms. Lyon's work appears on pages 32 and 50.

Other material compiled by:
Helen H. Moore, Kelly Boyer Sagert, and Kelly Womer

Note: This book does not constitute the practice of medicine. If you have any health questions or concerns, the publisher suggests you consult your doctor.

Aromatherapy:

An Introduction

How easy it is to become lost in the intoxicating fragrance of a flower garden, the pungent awakening of spices and dried herbs, the crisp burst of scent from a freshly peeled orange, or the sweet intensity of a newly bloomed rose. Aroma has the power to inspire, sedate, energize, and entice.

Aroma is also a link to other times and places. The sharp, earthy smell of burning leaves recalls dis-

tant autumns; the aroma of gingerbread cookies conjures childhood memories; and the lingering perfume of a lover's scent summons the warm clasp of a close embrace.

Aroma means scent, but it has powers beyond those that arouse or arrest the senses. Within the fragrances of aromatic plants are substances that improve health, promote healing, and support your general well-being. These substances are found in the plant's essential oils, which are responsible for its unique fragrance as well as its healing benefits.

But aromatherapy doesn't work by the sense of smell alone. Essential oils can be used topically, taking direct action on surrounding tissues and entering the bloodstream to be carried throughout the body.

The modern world has newly discovered the enchanting magic of aroma as well as the potent healing gifts contained in essential oils. These gifts, though, have been used by mankind at least since biblical times, and probably before. Today we understand why and how essential oils treat psychological and physical illness. In ancient times, people just knew that they worked.

THE ANCIENT MEANING AND USE OF SCENT

Mysterious, invisible, and deeply moving, aroma was long believed to hold the soul of a plant, to be the essence of the divine. The Egyptians believed the

fleeting scent of a plant was a metaphor for the human soul. Ancient peoples believed deities would find prayers more pleasing when sweetly scented, and so the musky wisps of incense were used in nearly every culture to carry prayers heavenward. The ancients surrounded themselves with the richness of aroma, believing that as scented air entered their lungs and pores, a link was forged to the divine. In ancient Greece, oracles inhaled incense scented with bay leaves to inspire their visions, and Tibetan women captured aromatic clouds of cedar smoke to propel them into prophecy. Purifiers of body and soul, fragrant billows of smoke were also used to induce tranquility, insight, intoxication, and inner peace.

Ancient peoples also learned that heated animal fats could absorb the aromatic properties of fragrant flowers and leaves. When cooled, such concoctions were found to help heal wounds, soothe sore muscles, protect skin from the elements, and add a scent of mystery and allure to the wearer. It was later discovered that fragrance could be held in water as well, either to be ingested as a tonic or applied as scent to the skin and hair.

The Egyptians were famous for their scented oils. So masterfully did they blend essential oils that calcite pots once filled with their scented creations still held a faint aroma when the tomb of King Tutankhamen was opened 3,000 years later. The Romans bathed in fragrance, while the Greeks generously applied scented oils to their bodies. The East Indians turned the use of scent into a sensual art form. Women anointed their glistening, freshly bathed bodies with jasmine, sweet patchouli, amber, musk, sandalwood, and saffron. Each part of the body held a different scent, an aromatic garden of earthly delights.

The bewitching aspects of aroma are as old as the entanglement of love and power. Cleopatra lured Mark Anthony as her slaves burned incense and fanned the smoke into the sails of her ship. When the Queen of Sheba made her famous visit to King Solomon, it was to discuss the trading of fragrant resins. Delicately scented smoke was used to perfume

a woman's hair
in ancient Japan,
and geishas
measured their
customer's stay
by the number
of incense sticks
that were burned.

Ancient Athens was famous for merchants selling enticingly scented body oils, musks, aromatic perfumes, and disks of fragrant incense. The Phoenicians traded exotic wares of Chinese camphor, Indian cinnamon, and sandalwood. Aromatics merchants from India and Persia carried jasmine-scented sesame oil to China, while rosewater was mixed into the mortar used to build sacred mosques in the East. So was the world once connected by the pervasive and persuasive power of fragrance.

Aromatherapy Today

Today, aromatherapy has come of age. Offering not only sensual pleasure but a fragrant cure, essential oils are once again being used for their health benefits.

Enter, then, the provocative world of aroma with its incredible diversity of scent, from the seductive richness of jasmine to the sweet gentleness of lavender, from the tangy scent of citrus to the floral purity of rose. Whether you choose a scent to invigorate and exhilarate or refresh and soothe, aromatherapy is an exquisite journey into body, mind, and soul.

LAVENDER

With a slender
stalk and lofty
spikes of radiant
purple flowers,
lavender grows in
lush fields high on
the sunny slopes
of mountainous
terrain. The sweet

scent of lavender is exceptionally fresh, as if infused
with the growing area's resplendent light, cool air, and
sundrenched soil. Though aromatic lavender is among
the most useful and versatile of all essences, the oil is
most renowned for its ability to soothe and relax.

Lavender is a hardy shrub indigenous to the mountains of Mediterranean Europe. Actually a member of the mint family, the luxuriant lavender shrub grows to an average height of three feet. Lavender's leaves are narrow, and the tips of the plant's tall spikes bear flowers ranging in color from pale purple to gray-blue to a deep purplish blue.

Though lavender's aroma is found throughout the plant, the essential oil can only be extracted from its diminutive flowers. The tiny blooms are picked at the height of their potency, usually in mid-summer, when the oil is fully concentrated in the flowers.

Many varieties of lavender are grown, but English lavender (*Lavandula angustifolia* or *Lavandula officinalis*) is true lavender. The French variety is the oldest and most highly prized.

A Christian legend says that lavender originally had no scent. Ever since the Virgin  Mary dried Jesus' swaddling clothes on a lavender bush, however, it has had a heavenly fragrance.

The ancient Romans were among the first to discover the aromatic joys of lavender, using the brightly colored herb to scent and purify their bath-water. The refreshing fragrance quickly became their favorite, especially for bathing, and it was for this reason the flower was named lavender, from the Latin *lavare*, meaning "to wash."

In Europe, bundled sprigs of dried lavender were burned in houses and country cottages to keep away

wandering malevolent spirits. Herbalists of the 17th century were enamored of lavender's benefits, listing among its therapeutic qualities: "restoreth lost speech," "healeth the swoonings," and "helpeth the passions and pantings of the heart." Due to these legendary healing properties, oil of lavender became known as the universal oil.

Throughout the centuries, lavender was associated both with relaxation and rejuvenation. Sachets made from dried lavender were inhaled to ease exhaustion and alleviate insomnia, as well as to treat irritability and depression. Victorian women used lavender-filled "swooning pillows" to revive themselves when they felt a faint coming on from wearing too-tight corsets. It was also believed that a daily sprinkling of lavender water, one of the oldest of English perfumes, would maintain purity and preserve chastity.

The fresh, soothing scent of lavender is now used to alleviate headaches of all kinds, from tension headaches to migraines. A few drops of lavender oil rubbed at the base of the skull or massaged gently into the temples will ease tension. A lavender-scented pillowcase not only encourages sleep but is said to prevent nightmares. Lavender also tones the nervous system, stabilizes mood swings, and soothes the respiratory system.

Lavender is sometimes used to boost immunity and, due to its gentle nature, is an ideal choice for children. In rural France, children are soaked in lavender-scented baths to keep them healthy. Lavender baths also fortify the immune system and stimulate circulation in adults. Just mix 8 to 10 drops of lavender oil into a warm bath.

A favorite ingredient in soaps and perfumes, lavender rejuvenates oily skin and eliminates skin blemishes, from acne to scars. It is thought that lavender may be a cell regenerator, as the oil has been shown to prevent scarring and stretch marks and even to slow the development of wrinkles.

Lavender has long been used to treat skin irritations, from wounds and rashes to sun damage and burns. In fact, French chemist René-Maurice Gattefossé plunged his hand into a vat of lavender oil after severely burning it in a laboratory explosion. The pain was eased immediately, but even more amazing was how quickly the hand healed. It was Gattefossé who coined the term aroma-therapy in 1928, linking the joy of scent to the therapeutic use of essential oils.

As lavender is extremely gentle, this oil is one of the few that can be applied undiluted, directly onto the skin. However, lavender is deceptively powerful. A few drops of the antiseptic oil on cuts and burns will kill bacteria, ease pain, and speed healing. Lavender is also beneficial for blisters, insect bites, and stings.

Lavender has traditionally been known to calm the heart, and modern users of lavender also find the scent stabilizes nervous feelings associated with troubled love. Lavender lowers blood pressure and brings forth a

deep, calming composure. Once commonly used to alleviate hysteria and panic, lavender works best on strong, even overwhelming emotions.

By soothing and relaxing pent-up energies, lavender eases feelings of frustration and exasperation. A quick sniff of lavender does wonders for irritability. Lavender also helps release stubborn mental energy, such as endless worry. In this sense, lavender helps to break habits, especially when they are the result of emotions that have failed to find expression.

Lavender encourages self-expression by promoting creativity. Reassuring and comforting, lavender is thus particularly suited to those who are oversensitive and shy. As we breathe deeply of this noble fragrance, lavender nudges along the beauty of our inner dreams, nourishing our potential and supporting our unique expression in the world.

SUNBURN SOOTHER

20 drops lavender oil
4 ounces aloe vera juice
200 IU vitamin E oil
1 tablespoon vinegar

Combine ingredients. Shake well before using. Keep this remedy in a spritzer bottle and use as often as needed. If you keep the spray in the refrigerator, the coolness will provide extra relief. For the best healing, make sure you use aloe vera juice and not drugstore gel. Apply as often as possible until you are healed.

HEADACHE-BE-GONE COMPRESS

5 drops lavender or eucalyptus oil
1 cup cold water

Add essential oil to water, and swish a soft cloth in it.
Wring out the cloth, lie down, and close your eyes.
Place the cloth over your forehead and eyes. Use
throughout the day, as often as you can.

ZZZZ FORMULA

15 drops bergamot oil
10 drops lavender
10 drops sandalwood oil
3 drops frankincense (expensive, so optional)
2 drops ylang ylang oil
4 ounces vegetable oil

Combine the ingredients and use as a massage oil, or
put 2 teaspoons in your bath. Feeling extravagant?
Then add 2 drops of your choice of an expensive
essential oil such as jasmine or rose. Without the

vegetable oil, this recipe is suitable for use in an aromatherapy diffuser, a simmering pan of water, or a potpourri cooker. Treat yourself every night before bed as a surefire way to drift sweetly off to the Land of Nod.

While with an eye made quiet by the power

Of harmony, and the deep power of joy,

We see into the life of things.

—WILLIAM WORDSWORTH

Peace comes dropping slow

Dropping from the veils of morning

To where the cricket sings.

— WILLIAM BUTLER YEATS

For every weary soul, there's a sandy beach to stroll

or a star sparkling in the night sky.

If you're far from the ocean,

or if street lights obscure the stars,

close your eyes and breathe quietly until sea and

heavens are born in your mind—

until you rest beside lapping waves and

sleep amid planets.

Last night the first chilly breeze

frosted the window

and the last red chrysanthemum

faded on the porch.

I languish in bed,

solitary and content,

as the season slips—gently,

simply—into winter,

the time of quiet regeneration.

What a thing it is to sit absolutely alone,

in the forest, at night, cherished by this

wonderful, unintelligible,

perfectly innocent speech,

the most comforting speech in the world,

the talk that rain makes by itself all over the ridges ...

—THOMAS MERTON

e

like the bird, who

Halting in his flight

On limb too slight

Feels it give way beneath him

Yet sings

Knowing he hath wings

—Victor Hugo

Spring's vivacity is not the only season of rebirth.

The shelter of winter, such a still, inward time,

offers a time for reflection and renewal.

When the skies dip more quickly into deep purple,

we move into winter's womb, growing quietly

toward our own rebirth.

The merest whisper caught inwardly can bring a
measure of confidence.

In the rush of life it might have gone unheeded;
in the quiet it has been heard.

—ELIZABETH YATES

Certain thoughts are prayers.

There are moments when, whatever be the attitude

of the body, the soul is on its knees.

—VICTOR HUGO

Always have something beautiful in sight,

even if it's just a daisy in a jelly glass.

—H. JACKSON BROWN, JR.

The true harvest of my daily life is
somewhat as intangible and indescribable as
the tints of morning or evening.
It is a little stardust caught, a segment of
the rainbow which I have clutched.

—HENRY DAVID THOREAU

Listening to our hearts gives us a sense of direction

even when the road is not well marked.

—Andrea Van Steenhouse, Ph.D.

After the rain all night,

the gray heron lifts from the fog

over the pond behind the house.

I ask you, heron, raise my hope,

and bear my heart aboard your tender wings.

This way, I'm sure the fog will depart this morning.

Consider a lilac blossom:

Each tiny, individual flower—

like an aspect of one's self—

must burst open its own radiance

before its hundred-fold bloom matures

full and fragrant.

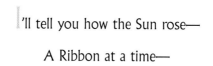

I'll tell you how the Sun rose—

A Ribbon at a time—

—EMILY DICKINSON

Returning to solitude,

that meadowland for hearts,

allows fruit to be borne,

for fields left fallow to rest

yield richest harvest.

For oft, when on my couch I lie

In vacant or in pensive mood,

They flash upon that inward eye

Which is the bliss of solitude ...

—WILLIAM WORDSWORTH

The holiest of all holidays are those

Kept by ourselves in silence and apart,

The secret anniversaries of the heart.

—HENRY WADSWORTH LONGFELLOW

Peace came to me when I began to

appreciate the color of the world,

the sound of laughter,

the miracle of changing seasons.

When I began to hear the affirmations

of beauty in music, and to enjoy the comforts

of hot tea by the fire.

—GLADYS TABER

Nothing contributes so much to tranquilize the mind as a steady purpose—a point on which the soul may fix its intellectual eye.

—Mary Wollstonecraft Shelley

It's raining here on the wooded riverbank,

to the delight of the cats asleep,

curled in a calico circle of quiet, on the windowsill.

They know the purpose of rainy days.

Between

the woods the afternoon

Is fallen in a golden swoon,

The sun looks down from quiet skies

To where a quiet water lies,

And silent trees stoop down to trees.

And there I saw a white swan make

Another white swan in the lake;

And, breast to breast, both motionless,

They waited for the wind's caress …

And all the water was at ease.

—A.A. MILNE

She loved the essential calm in the evening whiteness

of pillows, the plump welcoming, the downy

beckoning toward dreams and gentle slumber.

Look at that rainbow.

It is only when the sky cries

that you see the colors

in the light.

—T'AO-SHAN

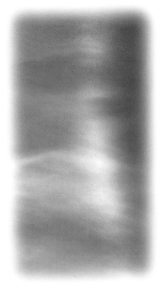

A tree doesn't ponder why it grows

a gnarled branch, a dog why one ear flops

half-mast, or a clover why it sprouts

three leaves, not four.

What is broken, mends;

what is stretched to the limit, strengthens.

That which is flawed glows

with certain beauty.

A thing of beauty is a joy for ever:

Its loveliness increases; it will never

Pass into nothingness; but still will keep

A bower quiet for us, and a sleep

Full of dreams, and health, and quiet breathing.

—JOHN KEATS

Let us imagine care of the soul, then, as an application of poetics to everyday life.

—THOMAS MOORE

Being a Soul gardener requires no green thumb,

just courage and persistence.

Never shirk from digging out your personal weeds

by the roots, yet be brave enough

to nurture the slim, timid stems to see

how they may flourish.

I am the daughter of Earth and Water,

And the nursling of the Sky;

I pass through the pores of the ocean and shores;

I change, but I cannot die.

—PERCY BYSSHE SHELLEY

The human heart has hidden treasure,

In secret kept, in silence sealed;

The thought, the hopes, the dreams, the pleasure,

Whose charms were broken if revealed.

—CHARLOTTE BRONTË

Night, when words fade and things come alive,

when the destructive analysis of day is done,

and all that is truly important becomes whole and

sound again. When man reassembles his fragmentary

self and grows with the calm of a tree.

—ANTOINE DE SAINT-EXUPÉRY

Permission Acknowledgments:

Page 30: by Thomas Merton, from *RAIDS ON THE UNSPEAKABLE*. Copyright © 1966 by The Abbey of Gethsemani, Inc. Reprinted by permission of New Directions Publishing Corp.

Page 40: Taken from poem #318 by Emily Dickinson. Reprinted by permission of the publishers and the Trustees of Amherst College, from *THE POEMS OF EMILY DICKINSON*, Thomas H. Johnson, ed., Cambridge, Mass: The Belknap Press of Harvard University Press, Copyright © 1951, 1955, 1979, 1983 by the President and Fellows of Harvard College.

Page 48: "The Mirror" by A.A. Milne, from *WHEN WE WERE VERY YOUNG* by A.A. Milne, illustrations by E. H. Shepard. Copyright © 1924 by E.P. Dutton, renewed 1952 by A.A. Milne. Used by permission of Dutton Children's Books, a division of Penguin Putnam.

Picture credits:

Cover illustration: **Elizabeth Golz Rush**

FPG International: Josef Beck: 53; Willard Clay: 34; Color Box: 18; Art De Oca Montes: 8; Farrell Grehan: 10; Kit Latham: 56; Barbara Leslie: 7; Planet Earth Pictures: 47; Ken Ross: 57; David Sacks: 35; Gail Shumway: 49; Steve Smith: 58; Andrea Sperling: 50; Telegraph Colour Library: 26, 61; John Terence Turner: 51; Toyohiro Yamada: 33; **J. Lotter Gurling/Tom Stack & Associates:** 36; **International Stock:** Mitch Diamond: 41; Chad Ehlers: 15, 54; David Noton: 25; Michael Von Ruber: 13; **Merrill Mason/Erik Landsberg Photography:** 29; **SuperStock:** 17, 27, 30, 31, 32, 38, 39, 42, 43, 45, 46, 59; David David Gallery, Philadelphia: 22, 40; Charles Neal: 55; Private Collection/Van Hoorick Fine Art: 37.